BARREN

Will you believe, in order to conceive?

God Bless
You :)

by Evangelist Danielle Williams-McCord

Barren

The Danielle Williams-McCord Story
Copyright © 2019 by Danielle Williams-McCord.

ISBN: 9781084199934
IMPRINT: Independently published

Printed in the United States of America

Meet the Author

Evangelist Danielle Williams-McCord

Acknowledgments

First giving honor to God who is the love of my life. I have learned in my time here on earth that the very reason I breathe is because God loves me. Everything I have is because God loves me. Everything that I've survived is because God loves me. I'm able to have and share this testimony because God loves me. Love lifted me and it was love that brought forth my son.

I have prayed and asked God for different things along the way; not so much as material or physical, but more like protection and favor. However, there was one thing specifically that I asked, begged, pleaded, prayed and fasted for and that is my son and he heard my cry. I am and will forever be grateful and thankful for the blessing that I have received.

When I began in ministry, I would always cry out to God and say, "Here am I, send me. (Isaiah 6:8) I'll go, I'll do it, say it and tell it!" and I meant just that. I have shared my testimony in my first book, **From Porn To The Pulpit** and now I find myself writing another book sharing yet another testimony of the power of Jesus Christ. I've learned that my life has become an example or an open display if you will...and I'm ok with that.

To my husband, Ronald McCord, I thank you for choosing me to be your wife when so many people called you a fool because of my past. Thank you for sticking it out with me not knowing if I would ever be able to conceive. You showed me that it didn't matter what I did or where I came from. It didn't matter if I was able to give you the son that you always wanted, you made it clear that you just wanted me. You have been loyal, encouraging, prayerful, understanding and loving from day one. I couldn't imagine having anyone else by my side. I am forever indebted to you my love.

I want to thank every Preacher, Prophet and Friend who have constantly declared and decreed that I would give birth! It was many of you who knew and saw the sad countenance on my face, but neither of you allowed me to accept defeat. You not only gave encouraging words, but you spoke what thus said the Lord, even when I was too depressed to receive it. Your constant prayers and prophesies will never be forgotten. At times I wanted to give up because this journey was indeed painful, but it was always a prophetic voice speaking, pushing, motivating and encouraging me to not give up and for that I say thank you.

Now, to my wonderful haters whom I love so dearly. I never could understand how a woman could make fun of another woman for being unable to achieve one of life's biggest accomplishments and fulfillments. Being a mother was a desperate desire that you all knew I had and struggled with. The women that I shared my pain with threw it back in my face, in the midst of small arguments or disagreements. If you wanted to get 'one up' on me, congratulations you did; because that crushed me at the time. I never understood then how you all could be so cruel or what did I ever do to make you hit below the belt like that. However, I now realize that you were waiting for the moment to rip my heart out "sis", knowing nothing and I mean nothing gets under my skin other than the inability to produce and you waited for your moment to try to destroy me. Newsflash, it didn't work!

See, if you want to provoke God, try to take his place. When a mere human being tells another human being what they can and can't do, what they can't have and what they can't be, it provokes God to show you who's boss. The Bible says in Romans 3:4, let God be true, but every man a liar. Every lie and curse you spoke over my womb provoked God to move on my behalf. He had to show me that it was a lie. Remember when you laughed and said, "I would never be able to have a baby." He had to show me that the word he spoke over my life was true indeed, so thank you. Hugs and kisses from me and my son...

Table of Contents

Introduction

Infertility- inability to conceive children.

Barrenness- not producing or incapable of producing offspring; sterile, unproductive; unfruitful.

Miscarriage- the expulsion of a fetus from the womb before it is able to survive independently; spontaneously or as the result of an accident.

Abortion- the deliberate termination of a human pregnancy, most often performed during the first 28 weeks of pregnancy.

Stillbirth- the birth of an infant that has died in the womb (strictly, after having survived through at least the first 28 weeks of pregnancy, earlier instances being regarded as abortion or miscarriage.)

Can you identify with any of the above? I

1

can....with 3 out of 5. Reading it may send chills through your body as it did to me; because as you read it, you're then reminded of it. Reminded of the trauma, reminded of the pain and reminded of an experience that just didn't feel good. Losing a child or the inability to have one is an indescribable pain. A pain I'm a little too familiar with.

The pain first occurred when I was a young teenager and although it was a devastating blow, I wasn't as impacted as I was after I became an adult with a better understanding. As a teenager, I thought I lost a baby, I wasn't yet aware of my inability to have one.

No man, woman, or animal can identify with that kind of devastation unless, they too have experienced it. I have gone through every emotion you can think of as a result of feeling like I did something wrong. It was my fault, right? If I hadn't lived the lifestyle I once lived and let multiple men have their way with my body, then this wouldn't have happened, right? When I needed to place the blame elsewhere, I blamed God. My anger was towards him, as I often screamed, "why am I fighting to do what you commanded us to do which was to be fruitful and multiply!" Can you imagine begging to do what you're created to do? I was angry.

Angry with God, angry with myself, angry with the people that thought it was funny and angry with the doctors. The doctors particularly, because I didn't feel like they really wanted to help or assist me in this journey. I was just another patient who insurance was paying the bill. They were not concerned with the emotional, mental or physical strain that my body was constantly going through. Being told that I was infertile or unable to carry a child to full term, yet not trying to come up with ways to fix it. Don't tell me the problem and not give me the solution. I guess I was supposed to take this diagnosis and die. How dare I want to be fixed or disagree with their findings. I felt defeated, I felt misunderstood; I felt barren.

Nevertheless, I held on to my unwavering faith. In my anger, depression and feelings of defeat I still believed, even if it was the size of a mustard seed. No matter how dark it got I knew that God could not lie. Whatever he said has to happen, it has to come to past, so when I or you feel like there is no light at the end of the tunnel, be reminded of God's word. I'm not just referring to the Bible, but every word he gave you, whether personally or through the mouth of a Prophet.

Does it hurt? Yes. Will you want to give up? Yes. Is it frustrating? Yes, but giving up is not an option! When you truly are a believer, I mean a real one. I'm talking about come hell or high water I'm still trusting God kind of believer; you're spirit man won't even allow or except anything contrary to that. Even when you want to throw in the towel or proclaim that you are finished; something rises up on the inside like (in Jeremiah 20:9) when Jeremiah no longer wanted to make mention of his (God's) name or in other words quit, he then said it felt like fire shut up in his bones. When you have an assignment and yes birthing a baby, a business or a ministry is an assignment; you cannot quit or stop until the assignment is fulfilled.

I wrote this book because I am familiar with the pain of being barren; both naturally and spiritually. I understand the place you may currently be in. However, I also understand the miracle working power of God. I understand what and where faith can get you. I know what can happen when you don't give up or allow the enemy to pollute your belief system.

I finally gave birth, and not only did I birth babies in the spirit (my ministry assignments) despite the devil constantly trying to cause miscarriage or my frustration trying to abort the assignment; I gave birth in the natural. After years of feeling anger, depression, confusion, less than a woman I finally gave birth to what I feel the enemy tried to purposely block. There was purpose in me carrying my seed and where there is purpose, there is a demon trying to fight it.

The reason you haven't given birth is not because you have done something wrong, the question is where has your faith level been during the time of conception? What have you been speaking over your womb? What kind of negativity and defeat have you accepted into your life concerning your spiritual or natural baby? You can and will give birth, there is just a method you'll have to use that a natural doctor can't give.

Still need some convincing? Well take a look at my journey and at the end of it, I believe in my heart of hearts that you too will no longer be barren. Barren in your body, barren in your business or barren in your ministry.

My only question is, will you believe in order to conceive?

Chapter One

The Beginning

The first time I got pregnant, I was 13 years old. I laid in a motel room under a 27 yr. old pimp and soon after I became ill. I had no idea what it felt like to be pregnant; I just knew that a missed period and nausea after sex meant a baby on the way, in most cases. I went to a nearby clinic and it was confirmed through a urine test that I was with child. Obviously, as a naive 13 yr. old girl I was terrified. I immediately told the father and his initial response was, "It ain't mine!" I guess it was hard for him to believe or he was too dumb to know that after one quick, and I do mean quick, encounter I could get pregnant. After constantly explaining to him that I hadn't been with anyone else and that the baby was his, he suggested that I get an abortion. I am no fan of those at all, however given the circumstances I agreed to go against my feelings and beliefs because after all I was just a little girl. What in the world was I going to do with a baby in the 8th grade?

We scheduled the appointment and that morning when my mom dropped me off at school, I hid out of sight and waited for her to drive away. I walked right out of the school gate to a payphone a few blocks away. I called "Kye" repeatedly, but there was no answer. With tears streaming down my face, I walked back to school not knowing what my next move would be. Should I just tell my mom? Should I reschedule the appointment? I really didn't know. Once I got home there was still no word from Kye, so I just put the thought on the back burner hoping it would just go away. That's how young and uneducated I was, thinking if I just forgot about it a whole baby would disappear.

Another month passed and Kye decided to pop back up, but this time he had a different plan. He told me we should keep the baby and that we could be a family. I was shocked and a little scared, but excited because deep down inside I didn't want an abortion and I wanted Kye in the picture.

Later that day, we agreed to see each other, and I should've known something would ruin this reunion. He said, "the baby was a sign for us to be together pimping and hoeing." "What baby wouldn't want a pimp as a daddy? I'll take care of you while you're pregnant, but after that you gotta get on the track." I just sat there listening in pure disgust. Yes, I wanted a family, but I wasn't willing to be his prostitute for it. We were sitting in his car in front of my house, so without saying a word, I opened the car door and walked into the house as the tears streamed down my face.

Several months had passed and I felt my baby's first kick. It was the weirdest, yet most fulfilling thing you could ever feel. It was in that moment that all unsurety went away and I decided to keep my baby. Was I scared? Yes! However, I was ready to put my big girl panties on and face the music. I knew my mom would be disappointed and angry. I knew my future was looking a little foggy as a single, teen mom, but I was willing to take on this new life despite the consequences. Every time I felt the baby move it was like a reassurance that everything would be alright. My mind was made up and I went to sleep holding my growing belly.

The next day my mother dropped me off at school, I waited for her to pull off and I headed towards the clinic where I found out I was pregnant. I was approached by a Hispanic nurse and I informed her that I wanted to start prenatal care right away because I decided that I was keeping the baby and I was already 23 weeks along. As I waited in the lobby a sharp pain hit my back. When I stood up to get the nurse, my water broke and it was full of blood. Before I knew it, I was surrounded by paramedics and I was rushed to a nearby hospital. The nurses and doctors kept checking my cervix and telling me that I was going to give birth, but my only concern was that it was getting late and I needed to get home before I got in trouble. A social worker came in and told me that I was not leaving and she needed a number to call so she could tell my mother what was going on. I tried to knock her upside her head! I was not fully aware of the severity of the situation and wanted to leave and try again tomorrow. I headed for the door, but was stopped by security and the painful contractions that I was having. I finally cooperated and gave her my grandparents number.

About an hour later, my mom and grandma entered the room. Grandma ran to my side making sure I was ok while my mom moved slowly as the tears slid under the black sunglasses she was wearing. My mother is a very talkative woman, but this time was pure silence. I could see the hurt, confusion and concern in her eyes. All I could do was cry and scream, "I'm sorry!"

The contractions became unbearable and I had an urge to push. The nurse checked my cervix and felt the baby and told me to push. I gave it a go two times and there he was; but something was wrong. They told me that this was a stillbirth, but he was very much alive which gave me hope. I fell in love with him the moment I saw him. It was an indescribable feeling that I didn't want to go away and everyone in the room disappeared. I only saw him, I only wanted him. I didn't think about his father being a 27 yr. old pimp. I didn't think about the fact that I was 13 years old in the 8th grade. I didn't hear the doctors telling me that he wasn't going to make it. All I could do was be in the moment and that moment was the highlight of my life; until he took his last breath in my arms. I told my son I loved him, he smiled and his heart stopped beating. It was as if he was fighting to stay alive just to hear those words from his mother; and just like that the baby I was torn about all this time and finally decided to keep and love, died. A piece of me died that night as well.

After my mom and grandma left the hospital, I called Kye. I told him that I had just given birth to our son, but he passed away. He said,

"Dang, that's messed up, but what you tellin' me for?"

"I'm telling you because he's your son too, Kye!"

He laughed and said, "He ain't my son. You and him can both die!" Then he hung up.

I was in too much pain to even react, oh but it was coming.

If my son's death didn't teach me nothing else, it taught me to cherish life. Cherish life because it can end so abruptly. My baby was here for such a brief time and it was over in a blink of an eye because I was too scared to face it in the beginning. I felt wholeheartedly that this was my fault and it could have been prevented if I would've just been honest with my mom and grandparents when I found out. I beat myself up and I was depressed and hateful. Why him and not me was a constant question I asked God. I was in a state where I wanted to trade places with my baby because the pain was too unbearable. Seeing his precious face grow cold while I was left in this world was becoming too much for me to bare. My depression turned into anger and rage. I was no longer the little girl that entered that hospital. Whatever came out of me had me tripping hard.

Now 14 years old and wanting to fill the void, I became rebellious, defiant and promiscuous. I started sleeping with girls and boys. I soon realized girls couldn't get me pregnant, so I doubled up on the boys. I slept with every penis I could find. White, Black, Mexican, tall or short, ugly, broke or busted I just needed sperm. I was determined to have another baby. I didn't need the dad beyond conception because this was my baby and all we needed was each other. I didn't care if the guy would stick around or not, heck I didn't even care to know their last names. The only thing I needed them for was to procreate. I didn't care about the reputation that was building from my 'sex-capades' I was on a mission to fill my womb back up with life by any means necessary. I messed up the first time I wasn't going to mess up a second time. For almost a year, having another child had become a task. I went on my rampage for months and gained nothing, but negative results. After sex with random dudes didn't get me pregnant, I finally quit. My body was tired and I was over the disappointment. Not to mention, I found some sense and realized one of these men were going to give me something other than a baby and I was deathly afraid of STD's, so this nonsense came to an end, but I knew I still wanted a baby.

Truth is, I was searching for that feeling again. That feeling only a mother knows about. It's like when a crackhead takes his/her first hit. (don't laugh) I'm not a crackhead, but they say that first hit is the best one and they destroy themselves searching for that feeling again. I was destroying myself in the process of trying to experience that moment again. Although it was brief, it was absolutely amazing and only a mother can explain that feeling when you hold your baby for the first time. Only a mother knows how it feels to look their child in the eyes and I needed to feel that again because it's nothing like it. Unfortunately, I never did.

Until the demon, I mean Kye showed back up. It was five years later exactly when I saw his face again. Honestly, for years I thought about cussing him out or fighting him on sight because of how he treated me and my son, but when I saw him his charm made me stupid again. I had just turned 18 years old and I was out shopping when I ran into Kye at the Slauson Swap Meet in L.A. I couldn't stand that man, but something about him had me drawn in like a fool. Maybe it was the fact that we once shared a son and for some reason I felt like we had a weird bond. I felt connected to this human. Whatever it was, he was back and I couldn't resist his lies and charming way with words. He pretended to be so sorry and wanted to fix it. He said he owed me the world and I should just give him a chance to make everything better. I wanted to believe him even though I knew he was full of crap because I wasn't that little naïve 13 yr. old girl anymore. I knew he was running game, but I found myself sleeping with him again. This time it was more than once, it was actually quite often and shortly after, I became ill again. It wasn't flu like symptoms, but it was that pregnant sick. The throwing up and feeling off balanced sick. Without even taking a pregnancy test I knew it happened again. I called Kye to give him the "good news" and it was like dejavu as he uttered the same words five years ago, "Why you telling me? It's not mine."

Annoyed, yet I wasn't as devastated as before because I was 18 years old, living on my own and making my own money....in the Porn industry. So, who needed him? Not me. I really couldn't care less if Kye stuck around or not because I had my own, not to mention plenty of men who was ready and willing to play stepdaddy. I was in a financial position to take care of ten kids if I wanted to, money wasn't a problem, but my lifestyle was a different story. I was a porn star preparing to be a parent, a stripper getting ready to give birth. I was ecstatic about the baby, but in no way, shape or form was I ready to give up my lifestyle. How was I going to eat if I stopped "working"? You need food when you're pregnant, lots of it. How was I going to take care of the baby? You need money when you're pregnant and preparing to have a baby, so I kept working. Can you imagine stripping and doing porn sober? It was absolutely horrible, but I gave up the alcohol and drugs because that was the right thing to do for the baby; which made it unbearable to work. I hated my "job" when I was high, I really acted a fool when I was sober, now I'm sober and pregnant stripping and doing porn. I gave those people hell.

This pregnancy was different from the first one because I was a lot more ill this time. I know the nausea and vomiting is a part of the symptoms, but I didn't know if it was the baby or the drugs that I was detoxing from. Whatever it was, I was super sick. It was bittersweet though. I wasn't feeling my best, but I was happy about finally being pregnant, even if I was going to do it alone. Funny thing is Kye would call and harass me whenever the wind would blow. I figured he was irritated at my independence; me not needing or depending on him didn't sit well with him. He was a pimp, so he thrived off of a woman depending on him to take care of them. Unfortunately for him, I wasn't that chick. The streets taught me to depend on nobody, but myself. Kye would constantly ask me to confess about who's baby it was and why was I always trying to pin a baby on him. "First of all, boy shut up!" Was my response. "The baby is yours. End of discussion!" He would just call me a bunch of names and say it wasn't. Deep down inside I knew it was his, but truth is I wasn't as exclusive with him as before. I did porn for a living, so there was a possibility, however I was sexually active quite a bit within those five years and never got pregnant until I got back with Kye. He swore up and down I was pregnant by a male porn star, I didn't think so, but we will never know.

Before the evidence of my pregnancy was ever revealed I felt life leave my body as the blood flowed down my legs and the sharp pains in my lower back were unstoppable. Here I am, alone laid out on my bathroom floor losing yet another baby. I know my lifestyle wasn't the best, but I was making arrangements to stop hustling. That baby actually gave me the motivation I needed to clean up my act. I drank and did drugs up until I found out I was pregnant and then I completely stopped. I was thinking about going back to school once I started showing and couldn't dance anymore. I was happy about this baby, why did God take it from me! Some people would say I wasn't ready, but try telling that to my heart.

Fortunately, this one wasn't as physically traumatic as the first. I was only 8 or 9 weeks and didn't have to push out a whole baby this time, but the heart ache was still the same. I was left broken and crushed. At that time, it seemed like I lost any and everything that was good. A baby is a good thing and I had already lost two of them. Unlike the first time, I didn't allow myself to stay depressed for long, I just went into rebellion. My attitude got worse, I fought more, I did more drinking and drugs because that was my way of getting back at God. You know I was high and stupid. I thought destroying myself was me showing God who's boss. The further I get out of his will is going to hurt him and that's what a brain on dope thinks. He hurt me when he took my kids, so now I'm going to hurt him by living a life that's contrary to his plans for me; because that's what we do right. Get mad at God and act out aka destroy ourselves as if we are punishing him.

I continued in the porn industry and strip club until I had a brush with death for the last time. I encountered a man who tried to kill me in a New York basement. Being nineteen alone and at the mercy of someone crazy is enough for you to reevaluate your life. When I was in that basement, I begged God to let me live and if he did, I would change my life for him and that's exactly what I did.

I was able to escape New York and when I returned home, I began my healing and deliverance process. I was done with hustling, striping and the porn life. I made a vow to God and I was going to fulfill it because somebody needed to hear my story. Somebody needed to see an example of what God can do in their life. Not to mention, I was indebted to him for all he has done. I lived reckless and through every situation I know for a fact that God had his hand on my life, protecting me from every plan and plot of the enemy; and like any new relationship you want to brag about your partner. I wanted to brag about God, I was in love with him simply because he loved me first and showed it. I had to tell the world about him. Surviving all of my mistakes and bad choices gave me the authority to help, guide, assist and minister to others, so I went *from porn to the pulpit.*

Chapter Two

The Barreness

Before I dived into ministry, I was just a sold out Christian still making mistakes. See I love God, but old habits die hard and one of those habits were the type of men that I was attracted to. I was trying to transition from a lifestyle that I was accustomed to for so many years. I didn't know what kind of man was best for me when I've only encountered gangsters and scammers and that's what I thought I needed. Yes, I was in church, out of the porn industry and no longer dancing in the strip clubs, but I was in an unstable relationship with a thug. I was rough, so I thought that was what I needed. I felt like he was my protector because he sagged his pants, represented a hood that didn't belong to him and had a gun. I was still young and although street smart, I was very naïve in certain situations. "Spazz" was my first real boyfriend; all the other guys I encountered were just tricks, pimps and sugar daddies, but Spazz was my man with no terms and conditions. In other words, it didn't cost him an upfront fee to be with me.

I must've still been high on drugs to even get involved with him. I was 20 years old, he was pushing forty and still gang banging. He wasn't prince charming by any means, but I liked him because he was persistent and familiar. He wouldn't take no for an answer and pursued me non-stop until I finally gave in. He was also a familiar spirit with a personality and lifestyle that I was used to which was hood and ghetto. He made me laugh and I felt safe. He always wanted me around him and invited me to move in with him quickly. He bragged about me to his friends and I was hooked to the soul tie of his "thug passion".

We seemed to fit, although cheating and domestic violence was what came with this one. Not to mention, I found out about a wife and three kids. After being cheated on, beaten up and mistreated I could have left, but I didn't, I just played the same game and I was better at it. He hit me, so I punched holes in his walls and tore his house up. He cheated on me, so I gave men his address and they picked me up and took me on dates. This lasted for a while, until I decided that this was ignorant and instead of going tit for tat I should just leave, but the unexpected happened. Several months into our relationship I found out I was pregnant. We weren't using protection, but we weren't actively trying to conceive either. When I told Spazz, I immediately expected him to act a fool, tell me it isn't his, leave me, etc., but to my surprise he was happy. He said he wanted me to be his "baby mama" and he was excited that he trapped me. He wasn't who I dreamed of having a family with, but just being pregnant made me happy and it didn't really matter by who, as long as I was having a baby.

This was pregnancy #3 and it was already going better than the last two. I finally had the support of my child's father and although we were dysfunctional, unmarried and abusive we were in this together. I wasn't far enough to have a baby bump, but he would rub my belly and we would talk about names. We wanted to move and get a bigger place so the baby could have a nursery and not hear gun shots all night because we lived in the 'hood'. It was like the baby brought us closer because we argued and fought less and we seemed to be equally excited about our little one, but that came to an abrupt end when I caught him cheating again. I'm not proud of it, but I tried to knock his head off of his shoulders! We were expecting a child and he was out in these streets with wives and girlfriends; so we fought and the stress came. We weren't in a good place, but I still had my joy knowing I was with child.

Barren

Before I could make the announcement, I
started bleeding profusely. I was in denial that
I was having a miscarriage and kept telling
myself that bleeding was normal in the first
trimester, but that is false. Spotting is normal,
passing blood clots while pregnant is not. The
cramps soon followed and I found myself
losing yet another baby. When I went to the
doctor, they did an ultrasound and the baby
was no longer in the sac. You can imagine how
upset and hurt I was. Spazz seemed to be
saddened as well, he was my support system
during my grieving period, but deep down
inside I felt like he was relieved that he didn't
have to deal with a 4th child and yet another
baby mama.

Our relationship was already unstable and I
knew it couldn't survive this. I slowly
transitioned out of it as I got closer to God and
deeper into church. I don't know if it was love,
lust or stupidity, but knowing we were
irreparable I was still trying to fix what I knew
was broken and irreparable. If I couldn't fix
him, I knew God could, so I begged him to
worship with me and for us to take this godly

Journey together. Unfortunately, no matter how much I begged or pleaded with him, he was a thug with no intentions of changing. That was no longer working for me because I wanted a different life, which included more Jesus and celibacy until marriage. How can a man who was still secretly married and gangbanging understand my point of view? My relationship ended with Spazz, but my relationship with God was just getting started.

I had no desire for a man or a woman, I wanted celibacy and holiness. In fact, my body needed a break after the porn industry, prostitution and an abusive relationship. For a while, I didn't want sex. The thought of it irritated and angered me because sex equated to abuse, rape, infidelity and pain for me. I lost the desire for sex, but I started to desire marriage which I never wanted before. I just wanted to live for the Lord. I wanted him to use my story to deliver others and bring him glory. I found myself going through my healing and deliverance process fully and before I knew it, I was telling my testimony on the radio, television and in different churches. People wanted to hear from the 'ex-pornstar'. I believe my story was captivating for many different reasons.

I got invited to speak at a mega church in Los Angeles and there was a guest speaker who preached that evening. He was a big time Pastor of a mega church on the East Coast, as a matter of fact, he was my favorite Preacher. I watched him on TV often, so I was elated when he was so interested in my story. After he heard my testimony, he asked for my contact information and I was excited to give it to him. I didn't know what he was going to do with my number, I thought he was just being nice and was going to toss it in the trash the moment he walked out the door; so I asked for a picture like a fan and didn't think anything more about it. The next morning, my phone rang and I saw his name pop up on the caller ID! I almost fell out of the bed as I jumped up and cleared my throat of my man sounding morning voice.

"Hello!" I answered so frantically. He told me

that he read my entire book last night and he couldn't put it down and he was so proud of me and blah, blah, blah. He invited me to his mega church to tell my testimony and I was still in a state of shock. He was my favorite Pastor and he wants me to speak at his church. I quickly accepted and we set a date for my arrival. I flew out there honored and ecstatic at the opportunity. Once I mounted the platform to share my testimony, God moved and the people were set free. We had some good ole church that day and I thought that's where it started and ended, but we were just beginning.

I was shocked when I saw his number a few weeks later. He was in L.A speaking at a church not too far from my house and invited me to come out. Without hesitation, I got dressed and headed out to see the man of God. That man knows he can preach and he tore the church up! Shortly after it was over, I greeted him in the lobby and headed home. I got to my front door, looked at my phone and saw two missed calls and a text from the Preacher man. The text read, "Hey why did you leave? How far are you? Can you come back?" I quickly responded and said, "Of course!" My little gullible self thought that he may have wanted to introduce me to the Pastor of the church he just preached at, but the address he sent wasn't to the church or a restaurant, it was to a hotel.

Still unaware of what was about to take place I called from the lobby and said, "Hey! I'm here." He told me to "come up". Still dumb and naive I thought maybe all the Ministers were just in his room chilling or maybe he was going to suggest mentoring me since I'm a babe in Christ. Whatever I was thinking came to an abrupt halt because I was totally shocked and caught off guard when he opened the door in a bath robe. The man of God is in his drawls! My legs felt like bricks because I couldn't move them. He said, "Come in!" I don't know how I was able to move or how long it took because everything was in slow motion. I walked into the big extravagant, yet empty hotel suite and nervously sat on the couch. He flopped on the big king size bed and told me to come over.

Lord my hands were sweating and my heart was beating fast as I sat on the bed a few feet from this half naked Preacher I admired. For the first time ever, I was speechless. I didn't know what to say or do, so I just started mumbling about how he was my favorite Preacher and how I watch him on TV every day. I started talking about all these other big named Pastors and leaders who happened to be his friends, making sure I stuck to ministry and church conversations. He engaged for a few minutes, but he wasn't interested in that. He then asked me did I like him. I liked him as a Pastor, I liked watching him on TV because he had a lot of personality, so I said, "of course!" He responded and said, "prove it."

In my mind I was like um ok, not sure what you want me to do? A back flip? A somersault? The next thing I know, we were kissing. I was in shock, yet total euphoria because I was having an intimate moment with a man I idolized. He was my favorite Pastor, he encouraged and inspired me from afar for many years and now he's on top of me. He asked me if I had a condom. I said to myself,

Barren

"Um excuse me sir, what!? Do I look like I came here with condoms, we just left a revival! You know the one you just preached at? No, I don't have no condoms fool, I been celibate for a year. I thought you were going to pray for me not lay with me!" That was the quick conversation I had in my head as he waited for my response. I whispered, "No, I don't have any, do you?" He sighed and paused for a few seconds and then I guess he was determined to get what he wanted with or without a condom. That night, I had unprotected sex with the Pastor who spoke into my life and inspired me. He held me after we completed our intimacy and we fell asleep. I was awakened the next morning by a forehead kiss. As I opened my eyes, he was getting ready to leave and head to the next city to preach. I laid in bed confused, yet amazed. I thought I was about to become the First Lady of his church! I just knew we were going be together after this.

Every time he came to L.A we were together, he would wine and dine me, but I wondered why we weren't going any further. Seems like he was just fond of my bedroom antics only. I was just a babe in ministry, but church folks talk and as time was progressing this man's name kept coming up negatively. Everyone who mentioned his name had something negative to say which mainly consisted of his whore-ish ways. I was devastated as his reputation was being torn apart because I was under the impression that we were exclusive, only to find out I was one of many. I was turned off by the gossip because I knew most of it to be true. The whole time I thought we were courting for marriage being that he was the preacher man, but I was nothing more than his L.A chick. The icing on the cake was our last intimate encounter. In the middle of making lust, he became very vulgar and instead of turning me on, he was turning me off. I wasn't trying to be holier than thou because I was fornicating with this man, but I still expected him to be different from the thugs I was used to dating and he turned out to be worse.

I was no longer interested in being his L.A booty call, so I stopped answering the calls and texts, I declined the meet ups when he came to my city. Unfortunately, before I could fully remove myself, I missed my period. I took a pregnancy test and it was positive. Here we go again I said, but this time I was hoping that he and I would discuss marriage, being that we were about to have a baby and we, more so him at the time were very present in the church. He was in Africa preaching when I found out the results, I didn't want to call, so I texted him that I was pregnant. That man has never called me so fast and he was in a panic. For some reason, I thought that he would be much calmer in this situation being that he's been in quite a few of these scenarios before; allegedly there are multiple secret babies. However, I was hoping that we could discuss doing "the right thing" which was getting married and raising our baby together, because truth be told, I did care about him and I knew he could love me beyond sex. If he just gave us a chance, he would've fell in love with all of me and not just my body. I was dreaming and he quickly shut down my fairytale. As soon as I picked up the phone, he said, "What's your bank account information so I can send you the money to get rid of that asap."

I was speechless, I was shocked, I was numb. First of all, I don't do abortions, second of all, this can't be the world's favorite Pastor telling me to abort his baby! I told him we'll talk when he got back to the States, I hung up and then cried because I was so hurt and I felt used and worthless. I was celibate and content prior to meeting him, I was brand new to ministry and I fell for a "man of God" and we're not talking about just anybody, he was one of the top Preachers of that time and telling me to get rid of it. I'm very street smart, but when I got into church fully and entered ministry, I held Preachers to a higher standard. I expected them to be different from the "street dudes" I was used to dealing with. He really hurt my feelings and depression started to kick up. I'm pregnant, unmarried and in the church, but with all that being said, I knew an abortion was out of the question. I kept the pimp's baby and I was going to keep the Preacher's baby too!

Barren

I had an upcoming doctor's appointment, but before I could even make the appointment, I was awakened by a sharp pain in my side with blood protruding down my legs. My sheets were covered in blood and I crawled to my bathroom. I knew what was happening, but I was hoping it wasn't. I didn't go to the hospital, I just waited two days later for my appointment. The Pastor kept calling and texting me to get my bank information so he could send me the money for the abortion. Since I was fresh out the "game" I played him like he played me. I went ahead and gave him the account number, go ahead and pay me, but I'm still not getting an abortion was my attitude. He couldn't wait to put the money in my account and get the confirmation that the abortion was done. However, the doctor had confirmed I miscarried for the fourth time. Till this day he believes I aborted that baby, but in actuality I went shopping, so if you're reading this, thanks for the hair I bought and the bills I paid with your abortion money. You would think he would've been a little nicer and want to help me get further in ministry since I kept his little secret. Who knows, he may have, but I'm sure I would have had to spread my legs from Genesis to Revelation on a regular basis for this Preacher to help me.

I spent his money on what I wanted because I desperately needed a little pick me up. New hair and paid bills didn't do much though, especially since the doctor looked at my medical records and saw three previous miscarriages, now this being my fourth. She "checked me" and said that my cervix was tilted and weak. She said, because of that I might not be able to carry a baby to full term. There was no additional information or even a solution, she just sucker punched me in the throat with that information and sent me on my way. I don't think I was able to really grasp the severity of the situation because I was still very angry with the pimping Preacher and how he mishandled me, so I wasn't processing much at the time.

After that last go round, I was exhausted, drained and done. I had no desire to date or sleep with anyone else, because not only did I fear pregnancy at this point, I feared another heartbreak. I was just over men and any 'situation-ship' with them. I didn't want to engage with anybody, just me and Jesus like it was prior to the Pastor popping up. After that last miscarriage, I just gave up the want for a child. The doctor told me that I couldn't hold a baby to full term anyways, so why even try? Every pregnancy I had was with a no-good man that ended in a painful disaster anyway, so I was over it. The words of the doctor started to penetrate my spirit and I accepted being barren.

In the midst of "baby talk" once being asked if I wanted children, I would just respond with, "I don't want or like kids". After a while, I programmed myself to believe that I didn't want any children because that made it hurt less. I didn't want vs. I couldn't have was less painful. My reasonings would be that I just wanted to travel and that my ministry was my baby. I was very nonchalant when it came to the subject and would quickly switch topics. I eliminated the appetite for it and no longer put motherhood at the top of my priority list. I didn't even want to be married because what good would I be to a man if I was incapable of bearing his children was a constant thought. I scratched husband and babies off of the list as I buried myself more into ministry.

Chapter 3

The Brokenness

A few years passed and I was established in ministry. I traveled both nationally and internationally, made television and radio appearances in regards to my testimony and book, *'From Porn To The Pulpit".* I went on dates here and there, but nothing serious because ministry was pulling on me as I was booked regularly for human sex trafficking seminars one week and preaching revivals the next week. I think I was satisfied with a dinner date every now and then, to me it was just a free meal and a chance to get out of the house, but nothing more because I'd been through too much to allow myself to go any further. However, all of that soon changed.

I walked into the post office and there he was. This tall, dark and handsome gentleman. Our initial contact was very professional, he was good looking, but I wasn't interested in dating him in the beginning. I don't think he saw me in a romantic way either, but an unexpected friendship sparked. We laughed often and talked about our life experiences. He was a breath of fresh air, mainly because I was myself around him. We weren't dating so there was no need to keep secrets about my past or be nervous about what he'd think of me. We became close friends and he knew everything about me. One day he asked me to bring him my book so he could buy it. I brought it to him the next day, grateful that he wanted to show support, but I didn't think he would actually read it. I should've known something was up when he called me into his office a few days later. He wasn't being his normal silly self, he was serious which made me a little nervous, I didn't know what to expect next. He said, "I read your book. You been through a lot. Can I take you on a date?" A little puzzled, yet flattered I smiled. He said, "I just wanna be your superman and show you that not all men are bad." This man knew I was an ex-stripper and that I was once in the porn industry and still asked me on a date. I believe in that moment I fell in love with him. Dating other men after my transition was always difficult because I would be too embarrassed to tell them what I used to do and once I mustered up the strength to tell them, they either stopped talking to me or instantly wanted sex. I entered every dating situation with a secret, but not this time. We were friends first and we had no secrets because neither one of us thought we would be together. I agreed to go on a date with him. He swept me off my feet and proposed just a few months later. I had no clue that saying yes to a late-night dinner after work would equal to years of marriage, but it did!

Before I knew it, I was planning a wedding.

Barren

While Ronald and I were dating, we both had a clear understanding that we didn't want any children. He had daughters from a previous marriage, and I didn't "want" kids. That seemed to work for us. We just wanted to enjoy each other which included traveling, shopping, extravagant dinners and a whole lot of us. It was just the two of us and we had no intentions on changing that. I mean if I'd be honest, my husband spoiled me rotten and I was good with that. What woman wouldn't be.

I didn't tell my husband about the news I received from the doctor a few years back, but we did discuss birth control since pregnancy was not a desire for either of us. I started the pill because getting pregnant wasn't an issue, staying pregnant was. I was new to birth control and when you're on the pill it is recommended that you take the pill every day at the same time. Unfortunately, my schedule was a bit hectic and I wasn't consistent with the pill, so not long into our relationship I found myself pregnant again. Obviously, the circumstances were much different because I

I was in love and married this time, so it wasn't a disappointment or embarrassment. I broke the news to hubby by handing him a positive pregnancy test and I didn't receive the previous reaction that I was used to. Instead of the typical "it's not mine" or "what you gone do?" He embraced me with a hug and a forehead kiss.

This baby was not planned, but was definitely welcomed. We were hoping for a boy because he had no sons and I lost one, so we both were in agreement for a little man. We told a few relatives, but it was too soon to make a big announcement. Not to mention, my last pregnancies didn't end well. My husband was aware of the miscarriages, but not about my uterus being tilted and my cervix being weak. I just stayed in prayer, asking God to allow us to have this baby.

We were in love and although this relationship was still fairly new, we were beyond excited about our journey together, but before I could start looking at nursery photos, I went on a trip and felt that dreadful familiar pain in my lower back again. I knew what was about to happen, but it was just cramps, no blood and I was praying that it passed. I begged God for this baby because this time the scenario was right. This baby was unexpected, yet created in love and I just wanted the pain to stop. Unfortunately, the blood came days later as well. I wasn't with my husband at the time and I am losing our baby alone.

Ron and I didn't originally want to have children when we first met, but this loss hit hard and awakened something in the both of us. The thought of a family together was now a desire for the both of us and we decided to keep trying. I stopped my birth control completely and we were obviously intimate with no contraceptives. From that point on we kept trying...year after year, after year. Ron would try to ease my aching heart by buying Mother's Day cards from him and our make-believe baby.

I was a little annoyed and confused as to why I wasn't able to get pregnant after all these years of being with my husband. When we couldn't conceive on our own, we tried everything from Geritol to fertility teas and pills. I calculated my ovulation, I prayed and fasted, but still to no avail. I knew I had issues with pregnancy, but I was never diagnosed with anything (yet). I just thought that I would have to be on bed rest as soon as I got pregnant, but for some reason we were having trouble, which raised different concerns because I had no problems getting pregnant, staying pregnant was the problem until now.

I thought my troubles came to an end in April of 2017, my last menstrual cycle was right before our wedding anniversary in March, so when April rolled around and it didn't come, I automatically assumed that I was pregnant, but I didn't want to get my hopes up just yet, so I waited. May came around and still no period just nausea, sore breast and bloating. June was approaching which meant Father's Day and still no "Aunt Flo". I had to be pregnant! I had it all planned out and my announcement was going to be epic. My husband and I were going to go to church and then dinner, while a few friends decorated our home with baby balloons and I was going to give him a case with a positive pregnancy test in it. I knew for a fact that I was pregnant and this day was going to be amazing. On Father's Day morning, we all got up for church and when my husband wasn't paying attention, I ran into the guest bathroom to take the pregnancy test. My excitement quickly turned into devastation as my heart dropped when I saw the negative results. Is this some kind of sick joke! I had all the symptoms nausea, sore breast, bloating, cramping, dark blue veins in my breast, I was a crybaby, not to mention no cycle since March. I stood in that bathroom barely able to breath or contain my screams. I literally lost my breath as I felt my heart breaking, this made absolutely no sense. I made up a story about how I wasn't feeling well and couldn't go to church. I waited for everyone to leave the house and as soon as I heard their cars start, I let out a scream from the depths of my soul! I cried like someone died because I did die. I was so hurt, devastated and confused. I begged God for this baby and he allowed my body to play this sick trick on me. I literally had to catch my breath in between the screams. This felt unreal and cruel.

Once I calmed myself down, I still was in disbelief, the test had to be wrong. It had to be! I made an appointment for a blood test because I needed something absolute. Urine tests aren't always accurate, so I headed to a women's clinic. As I waited for the results, I built myself back up believing that the other tests were wrong and maybe it was just too early to tell. My symptoms were still there, so the blood test had to be positive. I waited anxiously to hear the news and a few days later they called me with the results. They were negative. Again, I refused to believe that! I have never gone three months without a cycle and I have never had these kind of symptoms unless I was pregnant, something is not adding up. Still not ready to accept the results I made an appointment at Kaiser for an ultrasound. When I got there, I disrobed and BOOM! There was blood everywhere, my cycle decided to show up to the party. The doctor came in and with tears streaming down my face I explained to her what was going on. She said that this was not normal and suggested that I do some testing. I agreed because something was definitely wrong.

She sent me to a lab to take an HSG Test which was the worst decision I've ever made. I laid on that table and let those doctors torture me. My cervix was completely shut and they couldn't get in after forcefully sticking different objects in me. They stuck needles in my cervix and then clamped my uterus down so they could insert this dye in to see if my fallopian tubes were blocked; all while awake with no medication. It was the worst pain ever. One of the nurse's there was scared that I was going to pass out from the pain as my body seemed to be going into shock. She placed a cold towel on my forehead to keep me conscience and held my hand doing this "procedure". Talking about she felt bad, she should've! Those folks acted like I owed them money the way they handled me.

I laid on that table with tears running down

my face, not just because of the physical pain, but because of the emotional and spiritual agony. I laid there in this position asking God why? Why do I have to go through all of this to conceive a child? It's so many women who get pregnant and don't want their babies, but I am ready to love a child and raise them in your will, so why do I have to go through this? You told us to be fruitful and multiply and I'm trying to do that, but here I lay on a cold table with my uterus being poked. When it was over, they helped me off the table as the blood streamed down my legs. I had to be put in a wheelchair because I couldn't walk out of the hospital. They placed me on bedrest for two days with pain medication. I stayed in bed constantly crying and confused while my phone was ringing off the hook for prayer requests and preaching engagements. I had to preach and pray for others while I was fighting this secret battle.

My husband and I waited for the results of the test and they were not what we wanted to hear. My fallopian tubes were not blocked, but I was diagnosed with Secondary Infertility.

Barren

The doctor also told me that I didn't ovulate at all. We know that in order to get pregnant a woman must ovulate, well I did not and who knows when this started. She didn't offer much of a solution other than to try IVF or adoption as an alternative. That night I was broken and the "old man" rose up. I drove to the liquor store, had to google one since I hadn't been in a while. When I found the nearest one, I drove there crying angry tears. I walked in looking like I was out of my mind and out of place because I didn't know what to buy. I forgot what I used to like to drink, so I just picked up the first three bottles I saw. I went back home and sat the bottles on the kitchen counter then went in my room and laid down. Those bottles sat there until my husband through them out. I just wasted my little money because my plan to get drunk and pass out didn't work. I think I wanted the liquor to make me feel numb, but truth is I was already numb.

I was heartbroken, I felt less than a woman because I couldn't give my husband a baby. I saw the desperation every time he looked at a father with his son and I couldn't handle it. He wasn't like the rest of the men who never planned a family with me and when I got pregnant, they instantly denied it or wanted me to abort. This man grabbed my hand at night and prayed for God to bless us with a son not knowing I was crying in the pillow every time he prayed that prayer. We aren't perfect, but we are perfect for each other, he covers me in prayer, we fast and believe God together so why so much pain? Depression was settling in, but so was anger. I was praying for women and men who were infertile and receiving praise reports that they were blessed with a baby while I was still infertile. I asked God how am I laying hands and prophesying to people with the same issue as me and they are coming out healed and blessed while I continue to bleed? I was preaching while being broken and barren.

Not to mention, my "frenemies" took a jab at my pain. It wasn't a secret to those close to me that I was infertile and that it was the most disheartening thing I've ever faced. I was the only one in the group who was childless, so I loved on everyone else's baby as if they were my own. However, as soon as we had a disagreement or fallen out, the first thing they would bring up is the fact that I couldn't have a baby. I guess they knew calling me out of my name wouldn't phase me and they needed to cut deep. They laughed at me and taunted me with it. I can't understand how a woman could make fun of another woman's inability to conceive. Not only would they throw my barrenness in my face, they would hit below the belt and not allow me to see their children after I had fallen in love and formed a relationship with the babies. I guess I could understand because how would I be able to continue a relationship with the kids if I threatened to kill the mama's.

My in-laws would also make comments about us not having children. When Ron would bring up us having a baby they would say, "You know Danielle can't have kids." He would respond by saying that maybe he was the problem and it wasn't me and they would say, "Yeah right, you have children. She's the one that can't hold a baby." I really wanted to cuss them out, saved and all, but some things cut so deep that you can't even respond.

I also questioned the Prophets who prophesied that my baby was coming. For years, even before I knew that there was an actual problem, all these Prophets would give me a word about having children. I would look forward to getting a word confirming that I would get pregnant because that was my only hope. Every time a Preacher wanted to speak to me prophetically, I was praying that a baby was somewhere in there and it was, but where the heck is the baby? Were they prophe-lying instead of prophesying! I know the Word says that God can't lie, but they smelled like liars because the prophecies didn't add up to the current situation. All these years, all these Prophets, all these tests and I'm still barren. I didn't need to hear another word, I needed to see the manifestation!

I wanted to quit ministry because I saw God perform miracles in everyone one else's life except mine and it built bitterness inside of me. I wasn't asking for a big house and a luxury car, all I wanted was a child and for some reason he closed my womb. Prior to being saved, I was getting pregnant left and right and although those pregnancies never went to full term, I still carried life in my womb even if it was for a second, but now it's a deserted, dead place. Was I not ready? Was I not going to be a good mother? Did he see something that I couldn't see? Why was I fighting to be fruitful! Was I being punished for my past? Is this my fault? Questions that went unanswered.

All these years in ministry, doing what God called me to do and although I'm not perfect I strive for perfection. I'm faithful even when I'm weary from all the trials, tribulations, betrayals and backstabbing's that come with ministry and there was only one request. I pray for everybody else's needs, wants, desire's, healing and deliverance. I dedicated my life to the Kingdom and I only had one request; a child. I wanted God to breathe life into my womb and bless my husband and I with want we wanted and no matter my pleas

Barren

or sacrifices it didn't happen. I felt like I lost
my strength, so I gave up.

Chapter four

The Blessing

I no longer researched natural ways to conceive because it was driving me crazy. I no longer discussed children or starting a family. Like most of my heartaches, I just swept it under the rug and buried myself into ministry; planning the next conference or theatrical production. My focus was geared towards everything else. When my husband brought up the baby conversation, I changed the subject or gave a nonchalant response. I suggested that we get a puppy as a replacement. Why did I marry a praying man? My husband sensed my spirit and grabbed my hands. He asked, "Do you trust God?" With an attitude I said, "yes." We prayed that night and something happened. It was like my husband gave my spirit man a jump. We came into agreement that night and I decided that I wasn't going to let the devil steal my promise! That's what he desires to do, snatch the promises of God. I knew that if God said it, it had to happen one way or another. The process was overwhelming, but I thank God for a husband who is a believer. I picked myself up and started the journey again,

We didn't want to do IVF because of the cost and it's no guarantee that you'll have a successful pregnancy. I wasn't going to pay thousands of dollars to gamble with my uterus; instead I continued with every natural fertility treatment, tea and whatever else I could find on the internet. My husband found vitamins that would increase his motility and sperm count. We continued to fast and pray, as well as stay as positive as possible. Things seemed to still be going at slow pace, so someone recommended a doctor by the name of Dr. Johnnie Johnson in Denver, Colorado. She said he specialized in women's health and he is the best. Since I tried just about everything else, I thought why not check him out too. It was only going to cost me a plane ticket to go and see what this man was talking about. I made my doctor's appointment and took a flight from Atlanta to Denver in November of 2017.

I walked into the doctor's office not knowing what to expect, yet hopeful that something good would I come out of this. Dr. Johnson examined me and found the problem right away. He did an ultrasound on my uterus and found multiple cyst on my ovaries. I had **PCOS** which is Polycystic Ovary Syndrome. **PCOS** is caused by an imbalance in the hormones in your brain and your ovaries. **PCOS** usually happens when a hormone called LH (from the pituitary gland) or levels of insulin (from the pancreas) are too high, which then causes the ovaries to make extra amounts of testosterone. Women with **PCOS** produce

Higher than normal amounts of male hormones. This hormone imbalance causes them to skip menstrual periods and makes it harder for them to get pregnant.

I was 29 years old and have had multiple pregnancies, seen numerous doctors and nobody told me what the problem was until now. All this unnecessary stress because no one took the time to examine me properly and find out the root of the issue. Dr. Johnson prescribed Metformin to help me ovulate and regulate my cycle because I was going months without one. I started taking it in January and if I be doggone, my cycle became normal! I flew back to Denver in March to see what else we could do. Dr. Johnson added HCG injections and Clomid. I took all three in April with hopes that I'd be pregnant in May. However, my cycle came May 3rd.

Seeing Dr. Johnson was my last resort, so once again I became overwhelmingly upset. I had a total meltdown, wondering why God was not allowing me to produce. I even suggested adoption to my husband because I wanted a baby that bad, even if I didn't birth it. While I was having yet another pity party, I remembered a scripture in **Proverbs 18:21** that says, death and life are in the power of the tongue and they that love it shall eat the fruit thereof; and then it dawned on me. I was guilty of speaking defeat over my womb. For years I came into agreement with being barren. I said that I couldn't have children and that I didn't want children, now I'm fighting to just have one. Our words are more powerful than we know, and I came into agreement with infertility way before I was ever diagnosed with anything. When I found the strength, I prayed and asked God to forgive me for the words that I spoke out of ignorance and pain. I asked him to give life where death has occurred. I said my prayers and left it alone. When they say let go and let God, that's exactly what I did. I didn't mention anything about infertility, nor did I have another 'woe is me' moment. I gave this thing to God and trusted the outcome.

My husband and I were supposed to do another treatment in May, but he was out of town during my ovulation window, so we skipped it. We were going to resume in June, but my cycle didn't come, which was normal because prior to Dr. Johnson I was irregular. It wasn't a big deal until, all of a sudden, I became ill. Nausea was the main thing, which should have raised some concerns being that I'm not a sickly person, but after my last episode exactly one year prior I didn't get my hopes up. A missed period and nausea wasn't enough for me to run out and get a pregnancy test, so I did nothing. Soon after, the headaches and cramps came as well, so I assumed my cycle was on the way. I tried to ignore these symptoms until the vomiting became unbearable. My mother texted me and said she had a dream about fish and was feeling nauseous, she insisted she wasn't pregnant, so it had to be me. My friends were aware of these symptoms as well and encouraged me to take a test. Yes, I wanted to desperately know, but I was scared of another let down. I didn't want to be disappointed again and my heart couldn't handle another blow.

As time went on the symptoms only grew worse. I couldn't keep any food down and the toilet was my new BFF since I had frequent urination. I had a little talk with God before I took any tests or made any appointments. With tears running down my face as I cried from the depth of my soul begging him to let this be the real deal. I promised that I would give this baby back to him and raise him or her in the will of God, just please give me this baby. I begged, I pleaded, and I cried all night as I asked God to bless me with this child.

The next morning, I found myself with four home pregnancy tests. I snuck into the guest bathroom with my heart racing. I used all four tests and then I sat on the bathroom floor, anxiously and nervously waiting for the results. I stood up about five minutes later and I gasped for air, my knees buckled, my hands shook as I saw four positive pregnancy tests! OMG, I am pregnant! God finally answered my desperate plea. I am carrying life in my body. I pressed my hands over my mouth so my husband wouldn't hear my screams and cries of excitement. His birthday was in three days and I wanted to give him the ultimate gift, so I had to keep this a secret.

I grabbed my purse and car keys, then headed for the door. I drove like a getaway driver after robbing a bank down the 75 freeway to my mom's house. I bust through her door and threw the pregnancy tests on her bed, calling her a grandma! We cried tears of joy because she knew how bad I wanted this. I was ecstatic and my mother lit up like a Christmas tree as we were getting ready to welcome a miracle to the family. The next three days were long and excruciating as I tried to keep this secret from my husband. When his birthday finally approached, we were joined by a few family members and friends at a restaurant in the Atlanta area. I handed him his birthday gift which was a pretty blue box with a pregnancy test in it. Once he opened it, he was shocked and caught off guard. He thought it was a joke and for the rest of the night he kept asking me was I serious. "Yes, I'm serious big head! We're having a baby!" was my response as I jumped in his arms full of excitement. I dreamed of this day!

Barren

Once reality kicked in, he became overwhelmed with happiness. We cried together many times after that moment, but nothing compared to our first doctor's appointment when we saw our baby on the ultrasound. I laid on the table and the tears fell as the nurse let me hear the baby's strong heartbeat. This was an absolute dream come true. We soon found out that God not only blessed us with a baby, but it was a BOY! We got exactly what we were praying for. I must admit that although I was overjoyed, I was also a nervous wreck. Nervous and a bit scared because I had never carried a child to full term; my anxiety kicked in.

Isn't that just like the saints to walk in fear or put God in a bubble as if he's unable. However, I am guilty of walking in fear. I feared that I would miscarry my blessing. Instead of moving forward I was stuck in the past, reliving my past traumas when God was trying to do a new thing. The enemy can smell fear and doubt, so he had a field day with my emotions. He tried to steal, kill and destroy what God gave me by planting seeds of death and defeat. I had a dream that the devil was going to try me, not just throughout my pregnancy, but during the delivery of my baby as well.

I was so scared of losing my son that I almost drove myself crazy. I went into hiding because I didn't want anyone to know that I was pregnant. I cancelled every preaching engagement and event. I didn't announce my pregnancy until the third and final trimester. In my mind, I thought I was being protective, but in reality I was operating in fear. Instead of publicly rejoicing and celebrating the miracle, I hid it. The specialists that I had to see were not easing my anxiety, they actually made it worse. I was considered high risk, so I had to see different specialist throughout my pregnancy. Instead of putting me at ease, they made my blood pressure go up and got on my last good nerve, as they constantly found something wrong with my baby. He was too small, his heart had a hole in it, his kidneys weren't developing right, he was going to have down-syndrome and blah, blah, blah. I mean give a 'sista' a break!

I know I had excellent insurance, so every time they needed to run tests, my insurance had to pay them. Ok I get it, the medical industry is about money, but they almost gave me a heart attack while trying to get a coin. What was supposed to be celebrated turned into a nightmare.

The doctors didn't want me to go past 39 weeks, so I was scheduled to be induced. Worse decision ever. After two and a half days of labor, my water finally broke. Induced contractions are worse than regular contractions and the man with the epidural was sleep. Seems like it took him forever to get in there, but once I received the epidural the pain ceased and my excitement started to build back up because I was about to behold my golden child! As much as I've been attacked, I should've known it wasn't going to be that easy.

I dilated to 6 and a half centimeters and then my doctor urgently entered the room. She put an oxygen mask on my face as she explained that I needed an emergency c-section. My son's heart rate dropped drastically and his head started swelling because I was too small and he couldn't fit through the birth canal. My doctor didn't think it was safe for either of us to continue with a vaginal birth because it would be a life or death situation. Here's my joy being snatched away from me again!

I knew what I was carrying was anointed and miraculous, so the enemy wasn't going to sit this one out. I didn't want a c-section by any means because of the many complications that can come with it, but Lord knows I didn't come this far to lose my baby. I was rushed to the operating room terrified, shaking and crying. I was reminded of the dream I had earlier in my pregnancy when I heard the devil say he was going to kill me in labor. In addition to that, so many women die while giving birth and I just didn't want to be cut. When I got in the room, it was cold and lonely. My mother wasn't allowed back there and my husband was getting suited up in his scrubs. There was one nurse already in there and I asked her to pray for me because I was petrified. She grabbed my hand and softly prayed in my ear as I went in and out of consciousness. Before I knew it, all the doctors were in there and it was time to get this party started.

I was under the impression that I wouldn't feel pain just pressure, but that was a lie! It hurt so bad that I thought I was going to die. The pain was unbearable and things got worse. I thought the liquid that was running down the side of my body was some sort of solution or water the doctor's were using, but it wasn't. It was my blood, squirting out of every crevice! My doctor said blood was coming from everywhere and when she tried to stop it in one area, it bled from another. My body went into shock and I kept going in and out. It seemed like forever, but they finally got the baby out and raised him up to my face. I couldn't even keep my eyes open long enough to see him. I didn't even know what he or who he looked like because I was delirious.

Before I knew it, I woke up in recovery. I lost half the blood in my body and my doctor strongly suggested a blood transfusion, but I declined. I kept saying, "I don't need a blood transfusion, I got the blood of Jesus!" "Well tell him to multiply it because you're low!" was her response. Even though she pleaded, my answer was still no. If all that wasn't enough, I swell up like the elephant man. I couldn't walk, I couldn't sit up, I couldn't do anything, but laugh at the devil. I went through hell and high water in the hospital, the enemy wanted to kill me and my baby, but we were here! I kept saying the weapon formed, but it didn't prosper.

I finally laid eyes on my son who we named, **Redeem Ronald McCord.** The feeling is one that can't be explained. My heart was running over with love and joy. Although, I was in physical pain, I was anemic, I could barely walk, I was holding my miracle! After all these years, tears, heartache, pain and prayers, I finally beheld a miracle and bore my son.

Chapter Five

The Prayer.
The Prophecy.
The Promise.

The Prayer: Most (spiritual) women who try to get pregnant but seem to be having a hard time in the beginning start to pray. When pregnancy is not happening as fast as you thought and before you ever suspect that there is a real problem or a medical issue, you ask God for assistance. Anytime something becomes a desire of your heart, you should pray for it to come to past. However, once frustration begins to enter in, prayer becomes less of an option. If we'd be honest, when we are mad with God the last thing that we do is pray. I'll speak for myself because there have been times during my journey that I couldn't find the words to talk to the Lord. Truth is, pain will put a muzzle on your mouth. We are taught to praise and pray through it, but in times of distress and despair we do the opposite and completely shut down in all spiritual aspects. That's more than understandable, but definitely detrimental at the same time. The importance of prayer should not be overshadowed by the woes of our lives.

Prayer is not just a form of worship, but it's direct communication with God himself. God, who is our source, should never be cut off from our communication with him in good times or bad, and especially while we are yearning to give birth not just to a child, but to anything we are set to achieve. The Bible says in *Matthew 7:7-8,* "Ask, and it will be given to you; seek, and you will find; knock, and it will be opened to you. For everyone who asks received, and he who seeks finds, and to him who knocks it will be opened." You can only achieve that through prayer.

Unfortunately, we have either forgotten that or our pain has put the significance of prayer on the back burner. Hate to break it to you, but that baby ain't coming if you don't first conceive it through intimacy with God. Everything happens in the spirit realm first before it manifests in the earth realm. Need I remind you, we are spiritual beings having a natural experience; so it must be birthed in the spirit first. The Bible says in *Matthew 18:18,* "Assuredly, I say to you, whatever you bind on earth will be bound in Heaven, and whatever you loose on earth will be loosed in Heaven." It has to be sent up if you want it to come down. It doesn't matter how devastating the news was that the doctor gave you. It doesn't matter how many negative results you received. It doesn't matter if you think you've tried everything and they have all failed. It will not happen until you fast and pray for it!

Because that is a signal to God that **A:** they really want this and **B:** despite the negative reports and outcomes their faith is still strong. Consistent prayer provokes God to move on your behalf. When you believe while everyone else is in doubt he'll move to prove that he is the great I AM that I AM and while they are telling you what will never happen, he'll show them who's in charge of your destiny, but don't shut him out by not pulling on him in your prayers!

I know it hurts but pray about it. I know it's frustrating but pray about it. I know it's been years but pray about it. Prayer still works and prayer changes things. Through prayer the impossible happens! Through prayer we start to see the manifestations of the desire of our hearts. Through prayer our faith increases, and Heaven has no choice, but to move! You have to push through the pain in order to see results.

I am a firm believer in prayer because I am a product of it. Even in my sin I had enough sense to pray. I was a whole heathen, but I prayed for God's protection and I believed that he would do it. The Bible says in *Matthew 21:31,* "Jesus said to them, Assuredly, I say to you that tax collectors and harlots enter the kingdom of God before you." It's because they will believe, sometimes more than the ones who proclaim to be saved. My question is will you believe in order to conceive? Will you stop walking in doubt and unbelief in spite of what you may physically see? The Bible says in *Hebrews 11:1,* "Now faith is the substance of things hoped for, the evidence of things not seen." You're too busy looking at the problem that you can't see the solution. The problem is in the barrenness, but the solution is in the prayer!

Philippians 4:6- Be anxious for nothing, but in everything by prayer and supplication, with thanksgiving, let your requests be made known to God.

Psalm 86:6- Give ear, O Lord, to my prayer; And attend to the voice of my supplications.

Colossians- Continue earnestly in prayer, being vigilant in it with thanksgiving.

Psalm 4:1- Hear me when I call, O God of my righteousness! You have relieved me in *my* distress; Have mercy on me, and hear my prayer.

Psalm 6:9- The LORD has heard my supplication; the LORD will receive my prayer.

Matthew 7-7:8- Ask, and it will be given to you; seek, and you will find; knock, and it will be opened to you. For everyone who asks receives, and he who seeks finds, and to him who knocks it will be opened.

Psalm 32:6- For this cause everyone who is godly shall pray to You in a time when You may be found.

James 5:13- Is anyone among you suffering? Let him pray.

Proverbs 15:29-The LORD *is* far from the wicked, but He hears the prayer of the righteous.

1 Thessalonians 5:17- Pray without ceasing.

Psalm 66:19- But certainly God has heard me; He has attended to the voice of my prayer.

1 Timothy 2:8- I desire therefore that the men pray everywhere, lifting up holy hands, without wrath and doubting.

Ephesians 6:18- Praying always with all prayer and supplication in the Spirit

Mark 11:24- Therefore I say to you, whatever things you ask when you pray, believe that you receive them, and you will have them.

Luke 18:1- Then He spoke a parable to them, that men always ought to pray and not lose heart

Psalm 55:17- Evening and morning and at noon I will pray, and cry aloud, And He shall hear my voice.

Jeremiah 29:12- Then you will call upon Me and go and pray to Me, and I will listen to you.

Isaiah 65:24- It shall come to pass that before they call, I will answer; and while they are still speaking, I will hear.

Romans 8:26- Likewise the Spirit also helps in our weaknesses. For we do not know what we should pray for as we ought, but the Spirit Himself makes intercession for us with groanings which cannot be uttered.

James 1:6- But let him ask in faith, with no doubting, for he who doubts is like a wave of the sea driven and tossed by the wind.

Psalm 5:3- My voice You shall hear in the morning, O LORD; in the morning I will direct it to You, and I will look up.

Psalm 143:1- Hear my prayer, O LORD, Give ear to my supplications! In Your faithfulness answer me, and in Your righteousness.

Acts 1:14- These all continued with one accord in prayer and supplication.

Romans 12:12- Rejoicing in hope, patient in tribulation, continuing steadfastly in prayer.

James 5:16- The effective, fervent prayer of a righteous man avails much.

Matthew 21:22- And whatever things you ask in prayer, believing, you will receive.

The Bible mentions a woman by the name of Hannah. I've identified with her in more ways than one. She was one out of two wives to her husband Elkanah. He adored and favored Hannah the most, but she was barren while his other wife Peninnah was fruitful in bearing his children. Although her husband showed her unconditional love and preferred her over the other one, she was still in agony about being childless, for God had closed her womb. Peninnah didn't make it any better, in fact she made things worse as she tormented and teased Hannah on a regular basis about not being able to conceive. I understand Hannah's pain, having to deal with your own thoughts, questions and insecurities about not being able to give your husband a child, but to watch a mean heffa like Peninnah birth baby after baby and throw it in your face every chance she gets adds salt to the wound.

Every year Elkanah would offer a sacrifice and give Peninnah and their children a portion, but because he favored Hannah, he would give her a double portion. I'm sure she felt the love of her husband as he did all he could to comfort her in her barrenness by implying that "he is better to her than ten sons," however it didn't fill the void. Hannah's sorrow had to be overwhelming as she watched her husband have "family time" and interact with his children that he had with a woman she despises. As someone who has been in her shoes, I'm sure she had to be more miserable than what the scriptures can describe.

Feeling heartbroken and inadequate, not to mention tired of being tormented, Hannah weeps continuously. She's so depressed that she stops eating. However, what I like about Hannah is even in the midst of her depression and agony, in the midst of being teased and talked about, instead of cursing Peninnah out and snatching her by her wig, (like most of us would have done,) she prayed! Hannah was hurt, but she prayed. Hannah was broken, but she prayed. Hannah did not allow her pain to stop her prayer. In fact, she prayed in her heart, moving her lips, but not releasing sound because it was her spirit that was crying out to God. She needed the Lord to hear her heart and not just her words. She was so deep in prayer that she didn't notice the Priest Eli was near. Hannah must've went in and became lost in prayer because the man of God thought she was drunk off that communion wine.

Hannah's Prayer (1 Samuel 1:10-11)

In her deep anguish Hannah prayed to
the LORD, weeping bitterly. And she made a
vow, saying, "LORD Almighty, if you will only
look on your servant's misery and
remember me, and not forget your servant
but give her a son, then I will give him to
the LORD for all the days of his life, and no
razor will ever be used on his head."

After she prayed and convinced the Priest that
she was not drunk, but simply pouring out her
soul before the Lord; he blessed her. Hannah
went her way and some theologians say not
even a year later, God remembered her, and
she conceived and bore a son.

Are you Hannah? Are you infertile? Have you
been struggling to conceive, yet watching
everyone else be fruitful? Are you asking God
when will it be your turn to give birth? If so, I
decree and declare that the Lord shall give
you the desires of your heart; if you pray!

There is also a woman named Rebekah who

was the wife of Isaac, and she too was a barren bride. The Bible says in *Genesis 25:21*, Isaac prayed to the LORD on behalf of his wife, because she was childless, infertile and barren. The LORD answered his prayer, and his wife Rebekah became pregnant.

I included those scriptures as a reminder of how important it is to pray, and I would advise you to quote and or memorize those scriptures and to incorporate them in your daily devotions and time spent with the Lord. I believe if we ask (pray) for anything and believe it without a shadow of doubt it will come to past. If you can see it in your head, you can hold it in your hands. I believe in the power of prayer, so I want to pray for you.

Heavenly Father, I come before you now thanking you for who you are. You are Alpha & Omega, you are all knowing God. You are powerful and you are a miracle worker. I honor you for your grace and mercy that you show us daily. Lord, I thank you for breathing life in what was once

dead and God because you worked a miracle for me, I'm believing that you will do the same for the person that is reading this now! Lord I ask that what was held up be released. I ask that you, being the life giver will place a heartbeat in their womb. Lord your Word says that let every man be a liar and let God be the truth, so Lord every negative report is a lie and we stand on the promises of God! I bind the spirit of barrenness, miscarriage and infertility and command them to birth in the name of Jesus. Father we pray for healing and deliverance of all the hurt, laughter, torture and torment from others who knew of their issue. Have mercy on them for they know not what they do. Lord I pray that you plant a seed in the womb of the person that's reading this and not just any seed, but a holy and healthy seed Lord. *Psalm 127:3* says, behold children are a heritage from the Lord, the fruit of the womb is a reward. Lord make them fruitful in all things! Open their wombs Lord, so that they can bring forth a child and even children. Father, even as Hannah was without a child, but through her faith and prayers, you gave her a son. Do the same for the one that is reading this right now. I call forth the son, I call forth the daughter, I call forth the twins in this season. Lord I thank you in advance that it is already done. I have enough faith to believe for the person that is reading this that their barren days are coming to an end. I have faith to believe that they shall be pregnant with greatness. You are a God of miracles, signs and wonders. Let what man called impossible be possible in the mighty name of Jesus. Even now God, infertility is drying up. PCOS is drying up. Endometriosis is drying up. Fibroids are drying up. Open up closed fallopian tubes, reverse every word curse spoken over their wombs and lives Lord. Now Satan, I command you to take your hands off of God's children in the name of Jesus! I break the assignment you have put together to hinder this pregnancy and childbirth. The blood of Jesus is against thee and you shall no longer interfere with the promises of God! Thank you, Father God for hearing, but also

answering our prayers in Jesus name, amen and it is so.

The Prophesy: I now understand what the fight all these years was about. Anytime God gives you a prophesy, you have to fight to get it to come to past. You have to war with that thing. Remember when Jacob wrestled with the Angel? (*Genesis 32:22-28*) He fought with him until he was blessed. There's a fight we have to go through to receive what is ours. The enemy hears your prophesies as well and he will fight you, so it doesn't come to pass. He will put all these obstacles and stumbling blocks in your way to get you to deny the power of your prophesies and denounce the power of God in your situation. What is prophesy? A prophesy or prophetic word is a message inspired by God, a divine revelation. The Bible says that prophets "spoke from God as they were moved by the Holy Spirit." The Lord will speak his Word through a Prophet specifically for you.

In *Genesis 18:10,* God used three men to prophecy to Abraham that Sarah (in her old age) would conceive a son. She birthed Jacob at the age of 90 years old.

In Kings *4:11-15*, Elisha prophesied to the Shunammite woman that she would conceive a son, although her husband was in old age.

The wife of Manoah remains nameless, but is identified as barren and childless in *Judges 13:2*. The Angel of the Lord appeared to her and prophesied saying, "Indeed now, you are barren and have borne no children, but you shall conceive and bear a son. Now therefore, please be careful not to drink wine or *similar* drink, and not to eat anything unclean. For behold, you shall conceive and bear a son. She later gives birth to the strongest man in the world, Samson.

There was an older woman who was also barren, her name is Elizabeth. In *Luke 1:11-15*, the Angel of the Lord appeared to her husband Zachariah and prophesied saying, "Do not be afraid, Zechariah; your prayer has been heard. Your wife Elizabeth will bear you a son, and you are to call him John. He will be a joy and delight to you, and many will rejoice because of his birth." Soon after that, Elizabeth gave birth to John the Baptist.

These women were barren, but through prayer and prophesy they were able to conceive. Each of these women bore sons and not just any little regular boys, but they birthed men of valor. They went through pain, torment, embarrassment and shame because what they were going to carry was heavier and more powerful than they could have imagined. When God releases his Word, it is so, however prophesy is conditional. You have to obey the terms and conditions for it to come to past. In other words, you have to not only be in agreement with the prophesy, but you have to do your part to make sure it comes to past. Pray, fast, decree, declare, cancel out all doubt, whatever you must do to protect the prophetic word you do it. Where we as believers make our biggest mistakes is when we no longer hold on to the prophesy because our process is painful. When God releases the Word over our lives, in that moment we receive it with joy and gladness until the enemy starts to release trials, tribulations and distractions in our lives. It's like we hold on to the prophesy with a tight grip, but as soon as you get a negative pregnancy test, the grip starts to loosen. When the doctor "diagnosis" you with any form of infertility, the grip begins to loosen. As time continues on and you don't see your manifestation within your timeframe, the grip begins to loosen. Although, it's not mentioned what these men or women continued to do after they received their prophesy, I'm almost positive that they not only received and rejoiced, but that they continued to pray and believe the Word that was released. Some theologians say when the three men prophesied to Abraham that Sarah would conceive a son, it didn't come to pass for almost 10 years! Time won't erase your promise.

I prophecy babies and blessings over your life! I speak full term pregnancies with no complications. You shall birth in the name of Jesus. Let every negative word spoken over your womb be null and void. You shall

be impregnated miraculously. You shall be fruitful and carry greatness. I command your partner's member's to align perfectly and your member's to align perfectly when you come together to create a new life. I pray that the Angel of the Lord be present in your bedroom. Let every man be a liar and God be the truth concerning his plans for you. I speak healing and wholeness to you and your partner. Even as you read and believe these words your body is lining up with the will of God. I prophesy sons, daughters, twins and multiples! I decree and declare your PCOS, Endometriosis, Fibroids, Cysts and closed Fallopian Tubes are being healed and will leave the doctor's astonished. Miracles and supernatural healings are taking place in your body now. Ovulation is occurring now. Fertility is occurring now. Sperm increases and motility are occurring now. I plead the blood of Jesus over every ailment in your body. I prophesy that in the season your body is preparing itself to conceive and give birth and it is so!

God has given me the authority and the gift to prophecy. I have operated in prophesy in my own life and the lives of others. The Lord didn't have me to write this book just to share my story about infertility, but I wrote this book to prophesy to your body and command it to conceive! God is no respecter of person's, what he did for me he can do it over and over again through anybody else that is willing to believe. Will you believe, in order to conceive? Will you believe in the prophetic word that was just released? Will you believe that God still operates in miracles and his miracle working power supersedes the doctor's report? The Bible reiterates the power of believing and/or having faith because without it nothing can take place. *Hebrews 11:6* says, "But without faith it is impossible to please Him, for he who comes to God must believe that He is, and that He is a rewarder of those who diligently seek Him." It won't do you any justice to read this book and still be in doubt. I understand it is hard to believe what seems to be impossible especially when you're dealing with medical facts. However, who's report will you believe?

The Promise: The promises of God are Yes and Amen! If he said it, it is so. The Lord is not a man that he should lie, nor the son of man that he should repent, if he said it, it will happen....if you believe! As I stated earlier, he will use prophecy to confirm the promises in your life. The Lord made promises to his people even when their situation didn't look promising. God made a promise to Abraham that he would be the father of many nations even when it didn't look possible. What has the Lord promised you? Did he promise that you'd be a mother or a father? If your answer is yes, then that's what you will be! Even if it doesn't happen naturally.

For those of you who have had hysterectomy's and things of that nature, where you feel it is absolutely physically impossible to conceive naturally, but God still called you a mother or father. Guess what, that is what you will be! The Lord can and will still bless you with a child even if it didn't come from your body and yet you will still have a natural love for the child as if you birthed him/her yourself. In *Exodus 2:1-8*, a Levite woman became pregnant with a son and hid him for three months and when she could no longer hide him, she put him in a basket in the Nile River. Pharaoh's daughter went to the Nile to bathe when she saw the basket, her servant grabbed the basket and saw the baby in it. He became her son and she named him, Moses. Pharaoh's daughter did not birth Moses, yet she loved him, nurtured him and raised him as her own.

There was also a man named Joseph, who married a young lady named Mary. Before he could lay with his virgin wife, the Angel of the Lord told him she would conceive a child through the Holy Ghost and he was not to lay with her until she gave birth. Joseph nurtured and cared for his wife during her pregnancy knowing the child was not his. Mary delivered the child and his name was Jesus the Christ! Although, Jesus is the Son of God, Joseph raised and loved him as his own. He became his natural father although he was not of his same DNA.

What am I saying? If you have been called barren or infertile and yet still believe God to make you a mother or a father, he can do it by any means necessary! Through your bloodline or through the bloodline of someone else he can still fulfill the promise! Once you conceive naturally or supernaturally, your child or children will be your reminder. A constant reminder of the prayer, the prophesy and the promise. My question is, will you believe in order to conceive?

Letter To My Son...

Dear sweet baby boy, I have never known a love like this. A love so pure and true. You don't know mommy's testimony yet and we will cross that bridge at the appointed time, but what I will tell you now is my years of heartbreak ended the moment I felt you in my womb. When I saw you on the ultrasound for the first time, daddy and I cried tears of joy. When I felt you move for the first time, I thanked our Lord and Savior Jesus Christ. When I held you in my arms, I felt like this was a dream that had finally come true. You, son are my promise reminder and every time I look at you, I'm reminded of the promises of

Barren

God. You are my answered prayer and every time I hold you, I connect to God even more knowing that my prayers never go unanswered. You are my miracle and every time you look me at me and smile, I am reminded of God's miracle working power!

As your mother, I vow to be your confidant. I vow to be there for you in your toughest times. I vow to be your best friend, teacher person Prophet and leader. I vow to instill values, morals and respect in you. I vow to show you what a healthy and loving marriage looks like between a husband and a wife. I vow to whoop your tail if you get out of line too.

You see son, your father and I waited a long time for you, we prayed for you to come, we fasted for your arrival. One time, we went 7 whole days with no food just water, I nearly died lol, but that's how bad we wanted you. I made a vow to God, that if he gave me you, I would give you back to him. I would raise you in his will and that's what I have been doing and will continue to do; because as much as

Barren

I'm obsessed with you, I know you don't belong to just me. You are an Angel that God loaned to me from Heaven and I have an obligation to fulfill concerning you. My responsibilities outside of feeding you and providing for you is to make sure that you know God on a personal and intimate level.

Redeem, mommy loves you with all of my heart and soul. I'm not sure how I lived life this long without you. As I write this letter to you, you're only 6 months old and yet you have a personality out of this world. You're so full of life, you're silly like mommy, you sleep with your mouth open like daddy. You're so active and alert, you love church lol. Most babies scream and holler after sitting too long in one place especially church, but not you. You act like you're in Chuck E. Cheese lol. I also know, you can see Angels, it's one in particular that you look at and talk to by the bedroom window. I guess that's your buddy because y'all be having a full-blown conversation and you just laugh and goo-goo-gaa-gaa forever. I know you ain't crazy, so it has to be and Angel you're talking to. We're so happy you're here.

Barren

I light up seeing you and daddy together, you two have a bond already and it warms my heart. He wanted a boy his whole life and he finally got you. You're his little BFF. I know for a fact he's going to teach you how to be a great man because that's exactly what he is.

As long as there is breath in my body, you'll never question my love or loyalty to you. You'll never feel alone because mama got your back! Son, know that we will push you to greatness, we will push you to your destiny and we will support your dreams, even if I don't agree with them. I want you to be a Preacher/Basketball player, but if you choose to be a Clown in a Circus, I'll never rain on your parade.

You are truly God sent, I call you my Angel baby because that is what and who you are. I'm sold out to the Lord and I preach the Gospel, but that doesn't stop real life issues and emotions from happening, but when sadness and frustration creep in, you smile at me and every issue vanishes. I don't like a lot of company, mommy is very "sometimey" and people get on my nerves, but you don't. I love having you around, you're my cuddle bunny. I am forever grateful to have you as my child and I will spend the rest of my days showing my gratitude to you and the Lord for your presence in my life. Redeem Ronald McCord, mommy loves you forever and a day...

Made in the USA
Lexington, KY
22 November 2019